Finally, the Moon

poems by

KIMBERLY K. WILLIAMS

STEPHEN F. AUSTIN STATE UNIVERSITY PRESS

2017

For more information:
Stephen F. Austin State University Press
P.O. Box 13007 SFA Station
Nacogdoches, Texas 75962
sfapress@sfasu.edu
www.sfasu.edu/sfapress

Book design: Thomas Sims
Cover design: Allyson Williams-Yee
Distributed by Texas A&M Consortium
www.tamupress.com

978-1-62288-156-7

Acknowledgments:

This book is the fruition of several years' work, and so many people have helped in its creation. First of all, gratitude goes to my parents, Frank and Elaine Williams, who fostered my passion for creativity, words, and language. They, along with my grandmother, Helen Kobylski, also showed me how to appreciate and love education. Second, thanks to my sister, Allyson Williams-Yee, for her cover art and her constant encouragement and inspiration in all things. And sincere appreciation goes to my MFA professors at UTEP who helped me with the evolution of my writing and this manuscript: Daniel Chacón, Jeff Sirkin, and Lex Williford, especially. Thanks to James E. Cherry for his unwavering insistence that I could do this. Also, here's a big shout out to M.L. Liebler who was my professor and first writing champion so many years ago at Wayne State University.

A hearty thanks to the incredibly inclusive creative writing community here in Phoenix, but especially to Jake Friedman, Shawnte Orion, and Kelsey Pinckney, who all make me a better person and poet just by their presence. Additionally, because my family lives across the country (except for my son), I wish to thank my co-worker friends in the Maricopa County Community College District whose love and support have made them like family for me: Mary Alpaugh, Jeff Baker, Renee Barstack, Laura Dodrill, Jenna Duncan, Jaime Herrera, Meghan Kennedy, Dawna Kremin, Autumn Bolin McKelvey, David Miller, David Munoz, David Nelson, Mary Jane Onnen. Renee Smith, John Ventola, Celeste Walls, and Laura White. Hugs and thanks to the rest of my Phoenix support system: Janelle Hills and Dan Ramirez. Finally, thanks for Christopher Laprath, who most generously and single-handedly changed my life.

Final thanks to Kimberly Verhines and Thomas Sims at Stephen F. Austin University Press for bringing theses pages to fruition.

CONTENTS

*To the father, Frank X. Williams
and the son, Andrew X.M. Robison*

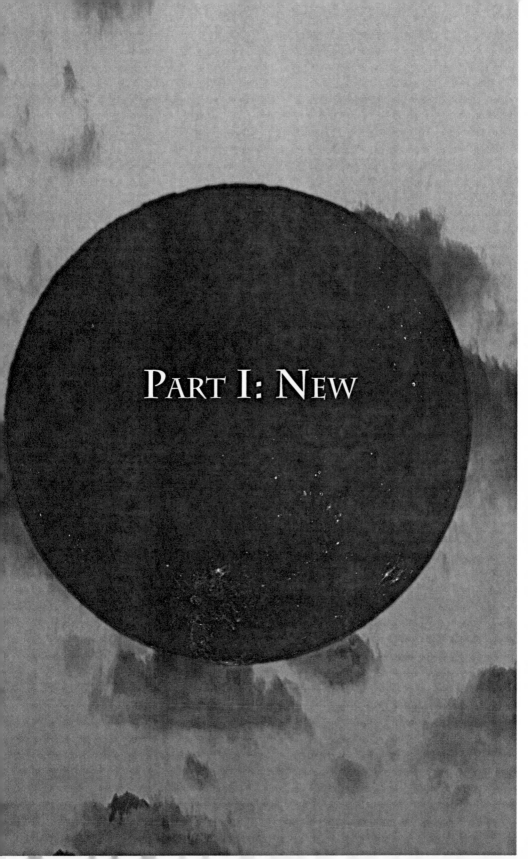

PART I: NEW

For the New Widow

While I am sitting under the cottonwoods,
thousands of cicadas
form a cloud of buzzing. My thoughts
are still as the grass,

the sky empty as a clean plate.
Andrew dreams the grim
reaper lives inside of him
and asks, "Mama, what does

this mean?" It's no longer
morning, and the day becomes
heat. Across the lawn,
the widow houses grief

while sitting at the picnic
table reading. Her eyes
water, but she loves
a good story. "Oh, you

believe in angels?" She
pats the bench twice, "Tell."

Sometimes an Angel

"La Paz is an extraordinary city, so near heaven, and with such thin air, that you can see the angels at dawn."
—Isabel Allende, *Paula*

"Do we take [Allende] for what she is really saying, or must we translate her images into metaphor and say that by 'seeing angels' what she really means is…"
—James Littleton, Professor

Sometimes an angel
is just an angel. It doesn't
matter if you see him
or not. It doesn't matter
if you believe. *How
can this passage be
read?* That sometimes
an angel is just an angel
ushering in the new day,
the lights of dawn glimmering
above the city before the sun alights
or perhaps acting as the good Samaritan
in disguise: he who slips one
evening into the streets like a London
fog to provide a cover
that helps someone find something
critical that's lost--a passport,
let's say, or a child--and who
disappears as soon as the air
clears, and the tourist, relieved,
starts for home. Sometimes
an angel is just an angel,
joining the mother in her
need, or offering company
to a lonely child or to the mother
of the child gone missing, providing
a light for the child lost

in the deep. Sometimes
an angel is just an angel. When
he arrives, standing
like a column beside
you, and he realizes he's
been abstracted into metaphor,
he'll likely guffaw, but you'll
hear only silence because
now there is nothing more
to hear and nothing more to say.

At 1:30 a.m.

Angels fill the house gathering
in the ceilings and upper walls
rousting about, describing how
we live inside the sleep

of the wounded. They tell me to love—
despite and even if. They give me
these words, pouring them like pebbles
into my cupped hands, and when I tell them

there's no love strong enough to make me
want to live in this world—not even
the love of my son, they say nothing
at first, so it must be something else.

Then they answer with silent ovation.
"You're so tired," they applaud. "Just wait."

Things We Can Talk About

My father, who recounts
funerals like he's telling the plot
of a movie, who combs
the obituaries more than his balding

head, has had a stroke at 72. My father,
who dominated a lifetime of conversations,
dwells in silence. The left side of his face
droops, and his blue eye tears. He's collapsed

into his six-foot frame as he shuffles through
life in beige moccasins. Before
I call him, I make a list, "Things
We Can Talk About": my aunt Mary,

the student who knows Neil Young,
the lack of faculty raises. As a fall
back, we can bitch about my ex-husband
together. My father, who recited

"Stopping by Woods" as if the words
waltzed in his mouth, who formed
"easy wind and downy flake" with his
teeth and tongue and lips, and made snow

appear with a wave of his hand, who
taught me to cherish sound as he read
to my sisters and me each night
before sleep, now sits as if he is

paused. Clots threaten where language
thrived. My father, heart of my language,
source of my lines, has finally run
out of words.

Do Not Touch: An Inquiry

Some of us need to dip our fingers into some kind of regret and walk around with them sticky for hours. What if I said you could only gaze at your lover? What if I said you can only listen to your favorite song on mute? Just seeing should be enough, but in Detroit I need

to determine if Rivera's mural is lively or tired, smooth or tough, soft or broken. Is the paint stiff or sorry? How does peeling and faded feel under tingling fingers? How can I tell by only looking? And in Oxford, I suppose that rubbing my front teeth against Thomas Bodalin's chest

to see how the wood holds up against humidity is also against the rules. Let me be clear: at the Prado, Calliope's nipples long to be brushed by a hand. Why else does her marble breast hover just above my head? Goya went deaf and Milton went blind. Imagine the vastness of that

kind of darkness. What would they do without their hands? How would Francisco meet the canvas? How would Milton find his daughter? How can light and air transform into life if all we can do is see and if we can never, ever touch?

What Remains

I. Song

My neighbor turns off his lawnmower. The grinding
noise gives way to birdsong. I make out five distinct
songs but can only identify one: the brown cowbird
gulps out his tune, sounding surprised at himself
every time. My guidebook says he is "to be discouraged
at the feeder" as he is "parasitic on" other birds.
I don't know what this means. So I let him eat

in return for his song. My yellow house faces north.
It's wrapped by green lawn and a chain link fence
that three does surmount on Saturday mornings
while I sleep. The cowbird's tree sits on the side
of the house where the grey cat presses herself against
the window screen, black eyes wide as dimes.

II. There Is Providence

On the front step, I find a song sparrow still on the porch
far from a window or a nest. The brown speckled
softness doesn't lie far from the feeder, so I cannot
determine how it died so close to my front door. I watch
the bad luck hover and grab my only shovel, red
plastic snow shovel, and convey the body across the street
to the hillside. As we cross, the bird turns from the wind

to face me, its eye spying me prepare its grave.
But the shovel's shape prevents digging, so
I must roll the bird under the sage, ease her against
the base of the plant. I sprinkle her feathers
with dirt, and what remains is to entwine
my fingers, fold my hands into wings, and pray.

On the Corner of Bedford Place and Bloomsbury

Not the leaves shaping
hands for the maple, not nighttime
dreams that suggest which side-
walk to take. Not even the green
air or the dog with his yellow
teeth vicious like love. And not the cries
of an infant, his open mouth like a baby
o. Not even silence, which you could
at least slip over your fingers like a glove.
What comes in this waiting? No words. No
letters to lend shape. No long line to run
down the page like a path carved among trees,
not the red letter post box or the shrill
sounds of traffic, buses looming two stories
high, running left along the road. Syllables
and clouds are frozen in the sky. Nothing
arrives but this space: white,
sullen, wide, and piled high with waiting.

.

Sweet Benediction

"Sweet is it, sweet is it
To sleep in the coolness
Of snug unawareness.
The dark hangs heavily
Over the eyes."
                —Gwendolyn Brooks "Truth"

Gwendolyn Brooks visited me
one night. She wore her large,
round spectacles, and her hair was not

yet gray. The room had one wall
of windows, which ushered in angled
sun and dancing dust. My students

sat around an antique table, their fore-
arms resting alongside the worn
grain of the wood. Gwendolyn Brooks,

who I cannot address in the familiar
as Gwendolyn, once asked, "Shall
we not flee into … the dear thick

shelter of the familiar?," had arrived.
She stepped around the table, placing
her palm over each student's

head as if we were playing a solemn
game of Duck, Duck, Goose. Pausing
she floated her palm through the golden

light above Katy's hair, and all remained
hushed, including me, including Gwendolyn
Brooks, and in the silence

of the pantomime, I realized when Gwendolyn
Brooks comes to say nothing, you listen.

An Essay on Refraction

Down by the river all
things are golden: the sun
in the southwest glances
off the tumbling river
and illuminates my son's hair.

Rain never comes
in October, except pouring
piles of yellow leaves. The dryness
comes. The darkness
comes. We turn back
the hour.

*

       The cottonwood extends
a hand blessing the river. The lower
trunk is the wrist fastened to the ground;
the main trunk profiles aligned fingers;
an artery forms the thumb. This hand holds
no human life.

             The female downy woodpecker
takes flight. Her underwings fan
out like a bloody sunset.

*

I have left the door open
again and let out the kitten
who gets lost coming home
from the neighbor's backyard.

*

The colors absorb my eyes:
Royal blue and gold,
then grey, grey, grey.

*

I am waving.

*

      When he goes, he leaves
the smell of coffee.

*

No one says,
"She's gaining weight. She must've lost
her poetry, again." But they do
assume he's walked out. Or she has no self-control. Or
she cannot manage her will. Or she must have made him leave. Or.

*

When winter comes,
she bathes in the leaves
that pile against
the fence.

      The boy cuts his tree, scissoring carefully
around the lines. It blazes red. The window frames
his effort.

*

These nights in my dreams
I walk and walk across
pavement, over exit ramps,
under viaducts--carrying
my sleep, gathering myself
around a spindle. I tuck in where
my esophagus meets my stomach just
beneath my breasts. I bundle
magic. I walk
and walk across miles of sage
and sand to where the concrete
wears the ocean and wait.

The Bodies Inside

Two bodies inside
the palo verde tree
outside the Walgreens
perform contemporary
dance. The male

figure, facing Glendale
Avenue, arches back while
spotting the female
who bends and releases
towards 43rd. They dance

in the wood chips near the bus
stop, where dark
exhaust emits clouds and street
people with shopping
baskets for homes shuffle between

the white lines. The palo verde
due south of the dancers
thinks, "I'm just a lowly
letter V." And the dancing
tree? It just dances.

Grace

The child works on printing, the fat black
crayon marking paper the color of the sun.
Upper case letters align like soldiers:

G G G G G G G G G
J J J J J J J J J J J
But lower case letters mis-

behave, reverse and drift: d d d d d b d d d b
                      p p p q q p p p p p q
She gets the first letter of her name

right every time: K K K K K K K K K,
but the last letter is tricky. Which way
to extend the leg on the v? And she wonders if

F is supposed to blow west
or east. Each letter forces finger
cramps. Her mother patiently

insists--again again--already teaching
the child the mystery of birth: the great
unease which leads to unwavering

devotion. Late one night, she accelerates
through the dark. Rounding the curves
of San Juan Boulevard reminds

her of the crayon tracing loops and filling
empty paper. She sees words
carved from darkness. All

that time at the antique desk
scraping shapes into letters, learning
reverence: letters to words, words to love.

Mexican Postcard

Why did I choose this one? Something
to hold onto,
the edges blue like seawater, and every
time I'm afraid of
leaving,
I am afraid of staying
I am afraid of losing
I am afraid of being
lost. I am afraid of
forgetting. And I am afraid to remember

Where every color,
every shape, line, every
turn in the card has
meaning and significance.
Orange jaguar dream, orange jaguar
crouched in
the turquoise field,
half-feline, half-human wearing
that wavy frown, sitting on
that throne, waiting for

the secret that's only whispered: *colors in Mexico are alive*, which comes while I'm standing on
the steps of Toniná looking over the whole empty emerald world.

About Angels

1.

Not moonlight, not firelight, not the vague
lamp of the TV room: none illuminates
enough to reveal the entire wing:
51 rows of 189 feathers.

2.

We older daughters were supposed to keep score
for all nine innings every game, but somewhere in the bottom
of the fourth, I left the remaining columns empty for about three decades.

3.

My father's crazy girlfriend thinks she's won, creating new
bank accounts and changing mailing addresses
for his checks, but she's the only one keeping

score. We three only want
our father to return to us.
                    What else do daughters want?

4.

I keep searching for the angel of baseball but he retired
during long the strike. He took off
his cleats and walked bare-
foot through the bull-
pen door in right
field, through
the empty
stands,
and out
into the night.

5.
Only the Los
Angeles Angels
really wear halos.

6.
Out of left field: the green
beans are in Bisia's silver
colander savoring the moonlight.

7.
On the pitching mound when an angel stretches his wings,
they grow the distance between first
and third--as the baseball flies.

8.
I count the wings that will carry me to see
my father--two wings per leg--Phoenix
to Houston, Houston to Detroit. When we

arrive in mid-November a gaggle of Canadian geese
will gather on the patch of green between Six
Mile and Haggerty. This is also along the path

we will take to visit my father. They'll make
six beaks, twelve webbed feet and a dozen
tucked wings all together. Together

my sisters and I form six ears and six eyes,
thirty feet and toes and a half-dozen grand-
children, half of whom are already grown.

9.
I imagine Cyrus on second, one wing stretched
toward first, one wing toward third. But he's facing
the outfield, and I'm behind home, unable to fathom his face.

Keeping Score

My job is to track each pitch and play, to mark
balls and strikes and HBPs—of which there are
many with these teams of eight-to-ten year-olds.
Every time my son stands at bat, his two front

teeth resembling side-by-side home plates,
I tally the results: ball one, called strike
one, strike two swinging, called ball two.
At the two-two count I breathe and say his name

and shout, "Come on, buddy!" But only once
in nine games has the outcome been any
different. That time he swung, and the ball
and bat together shouted, "Ping!"

and he was so surprised I had to holler at him
to run, and he ran, and I sat back down and picked
up the pencil and wrote: GO, 1 to 3, and then shaded
in the cross that marked the end of the inning.

Beginning

These little Sunday night
jaunts, throttling up Main Street
in the dark, dipping right on a yellow,
the wind fondling me beneath my blue
mechanic's jacket, gliding under the few
stars that outshine the city lights, my tangled

hair waving, and my lower lip
numbing as I cup his hips (the most
under-rated part of a man), I hope this isn't
the final ride of the season because the clock turned
back one hour last night, and now blackness escorts
us just beyond the city.

PART II: WAXING

On the Metro

What about the dark
angel? You know
him. He

enters the train wailing
like a siren, cracking
morning like a fallen

egg, demanding bread, only
a little bit of bread.
I clutch my bag

and stare like my Aunt
Georgine demanded I never
stare. I cannot

look away. Back
home, in the intersection
of I-17 and Bethany

Home, veterans hold up
cardboard messages
and one man waves

a sign asking for money
to visit his children
1500 miles away. I hand

dollars out the window.
But this one. I don't give
him a Euro nor the extra

nectarine the senora
packed into my sack.
Filth seals his toes

into curves that paw
through each car, each
step a cloven hoof placed

carefully inside
another body's shadow.

I Waited for Sunday to Return

I. On Saturday, in Nogales

I speak Spanish. It comes out swinging
like a rusty gate. We use the bathrooms in Food
City, and I buy a few *santos*, and when we go
to Payless for shoes for my son, the young man
behind the counter tries to upsell us in English,
but his gate gets stuck in the mud, so I say,
Podemos hablar en Español. He smiles
but remains silent in either language until
the paper curls out of the register and with
a flourish, he yanks it free and announces, *"el recebo."*

2. Later, the Drive

back to Tombstone is clear with showers of cottonwood
leaves. The road curves like my body—quickly
and unexpectedly with one or two pot holes paving
the way for the slight chance of utter collapse.

3. At the Ghost

town, we park on the outskirts and hike in.
Main Street boasts only dirt and weeds
waiting their turn to tumble. I peel white
paint off a wooden rail near the one-room
schoolhouse thinking that even
the angels have deserted. The sun
washes the day and clarity
stretches like a dome to the distant
stream. I want to ride the sunlight down
to the river and follow its flow but I, like
the weeds, am waiting for wind to sway me.

On Monday

Sunday arrived a day late. I always
forget how short she is and how big-eyed
she looks peeking over a stack of books,

and everything in the distance is just a little too far
away to be clear. Sometimes the sun glances
on my pages, transforming my hand

into a moving shadow, and then blue lines
appear from the dark. When Sunday arrives
on Monday, there's nothing to do
but find Tuesday and see if anyone else turns up.

Bull, Horse & Reclining Woman

I.

Who expects Picasso to turn
up in Glendale, hanging
between a Matisse
and a Miró? It's a sketch

not a painting from the Blue
period: dark
ink pen on paper
behind glass. It won't fetch

millions at auction, I'd wager,
but the fingertips that conjured
La Guernica lit this paper too.

II.

What route did it take to arrive
here and be fixed to a wall
in the suburban desert? Did
anyone say, "Someday, Pablo,

your horse and reclining woman will hang twenty
feet from palm trees and young people on cell-
phones who won't answer your call?"
And when they do glance at your twisting

horse, by chance walking
by, they will say, "Really?
I could draw that too."

III.

The librarian finds me in reference,
head tucked, writing

this poem, points
her finger and asks, "Is that your
student?" I nod. "He just used the Picasso
as a clipboard, *put his paper right
over the glass and wrote on it*. It's
a breech in etiquette,

you know." I know.
But at least he got to touch.

Pocket Poem

Digging through my purse I say, "I know I have a poem
in here somewhere." I pull out a compact, a tampon, a lipstick,
an opened roll of Mentos, the pink wallet I got for Mother's
Day, two postage stamps stuck back to back, my eyeglass
case, a packet of Kleenex, my iPod, an old granola
bar, an apple, one winter glove, a clanging clutch of car
keys, a plastic Tyrannosaurus Rex whose over-sized
tooth chomps my thumb, two pieces of Trident
gum slipped from their paper wraps, a rumpled Starbucks
coupon, a library note stamped "overdue," an empty
bottle of Aleve lined with lint, some dental floss,
frayed and unwound from its spool, a dried Sharpie
missing its cap, a Chicago Cubs pencil with a broken
tip, and one lone brown M&M, which I study
hard to see how edible it might be.

What Lies Ahead

Jesus Is Watching You says the billboard above
the adult video store. Every day, for seconds passing
by in the car, I watch him watch me: at first

we're acquaintances, and then, one day,
I'm ambushed by desire. (What would
the Buddha say—Jesus hovering over the adult

video store, churning up desire?). Oh Jesus,
with the watery eyes, Jesus, with the wavy, rock-
star hair and close beard that outlines thick

lips. His mouth forms the love I crave. As he peers
down from his billboard, we exchange glances.
He is the compassion I don't give myself,

the perceptive man I've yearned for
who comprehends my beauty and forgives
me my trespasses as I am unable

to forgive myself. Soon the video store
vanishes. I'm too taken with Jesus
who is no longer mounted mid-air

and I'm sure his cries arouse the dawn,
and I'm imagining his fingers brushing
my face, his tongue long between my lips.

And as I dream of loving Jesus, I am swerving,
nearly colliding with myself, completely ignoring the road.

In Sedona

I keep a flower in my pocket
and when I lift it out
it rains one yellow petal at a time.
When Andrew and I came

here in January only the clouds
kept us company along with
a little pattering rain. Today,
the vistas open 360 degrees.

Men walk by speaking
French and Spanish as Americans
shout from the top of the red
rocks. I sit beneath a shaggy

dream in the shade. Orange
flowers stir the wind. Juniper
nuts dot the earth. Later, I walk
by the piñon at the top of the vortex

whose branches wave and hand
me a message. When I arrive
at the bottom I find Andrew
holding a message, too, but we

stay silent. Neither
one of us knows what it means.

Finding St. Anthony

Святий Антоній
Святий Андрій
Святого Миколая

Dozens of saints lie under glass
coffins in the narrow passages
underneath Kiev. I am

uncertain which glass box with the Cyrillic spelling
contains Saint Anthony, so I pray before each
one: in gratitude,

Saint A., patron saint of lost
items (car keys, glasses, marriage
licenses, faith), the saint I need

the most, Patron Saint of Domestic
Animals and Children, pray for us -- all of us -- the whole
lot: four cats, three boys, two dogs. Oh,

and the parakeets, too. My beeswax candle
wavers, and the monk in the brown habit
gestures that I should catch the drippings.

I cannot pray hard
enough. Before each casket, I stop, bow
in thanks--the heat on my brow, my babushka

slipping down my silky hair: *Saint Anthony,*
thank you, and if you're not St. Anthony,
rest in peace, and please forgive the intrusion.

A Sonnet from the University of Alcalá

That day, Spain conspired against the tour
guide, whose choppy English succumbed
to the cacophony: the doves crying bullshit,
the sparrows bickering, the jet gunning
overhead. The crows shouted for silence so
they could cry alone. Lunch bags crinkled,
complaining of the weight of the ham, bread, and juice
inside them. We were here for a grand tour of history:
to see the where the holy seed of San Ignacio de Loyola
was planted, to marvel in the courtyard at the Latin
phrases that hovered like airplane advertisements far
above. But I only memorized the sounds shaking
like leaves in every direction, the guide who spoke
on mute, and the storks nesting quietly in the distance.

Nothing about Enough

That family in Nica—husband and wife
and their two children—all in one room
no larger than our kitchen, including
their table and comal and straw pallets,
and their coughing baby who had oceans
tossing in her lungs while mucus sealed
her eyes and lips. Her mother begged,
por favor. And my child now, so
insistent on headphones and cellphones
and devices to hold. St. Mary, mother
of God, how do we stop the wanting?

The manger is a just metaphor—our
children can be warmed by even
a donkey and celebrated by three
wise men—three should be enough.
But my own child, my own, the one
who drank my milk for twenty-two
months, knows nothing about enough.
No roof on the school in Nicaragua,
no books, no paper, no pens, not even
a pencil or a crayon to write a poem.
But he wants another one, just one, you
know, this time a different size or color.

Just Outside of Winslow

Sometimes your woes meet you sitting in the first bathroom
stall at the Flying J gas station with your purse balanced
on your knees, the brown wall sullied with black
marker: *Donny K. has a limp dick*, and scrawled
beneath in blue pen with a fat heart dotting *it*. *I know. He can't
get it up*. On the road back to the highway, you notice the Purina
store and note the second young couple you've seen in
one day holding up a cardboard sign on the side of the road:
"We'd rather beg than steal." You roll down
the window and hand them a five. Though right now,
you're still in stall one, hands clasped over your head, counting
up the numbers: hours on the road: four; months your eight year-old
son has lived half-way around the world: six; the number
of days until you return to work: three; the number of times
your new husband has been angry enough that he won't
forget your words: too many. Pouting in the back seat of the car
while he accelerates to ninety, you regress to the age when you
learned to manage long car rides, Detroit to Valhalla, twelve
hours each way for three-day stays before headphones, computer
games, and video systems littered the car, your growing
limbs allowed one-third of the back of the tiny orange
Horizon. As you calculate the number of hours until you arrive
in the valley, one lone cloud in the Arizona sky forms a top
hat, drifting along the high plains.

Finding Dziadzi

I try to find his stone in the cemetery
south of Detroit. The stepsons sit in the car, grumpy
about looking for the grave of a man they never knew.
I recall his mound and marker sitting under a pine

with no one else beside him, and I find his parents where
they're supposed to be, closer to the road. Why isn't my grandfather
buried near his parents? After he died, my grandmother changed
her mind and decided on cremation. Her dust floats in the sun-

light in the aspens outside Pagosa Springs, so far from downriver
Detroit. In the meantime, I've lost Dziadzi in the twenty-three
years of stones and graves added around his narrow spot.
I call my mother who tells me what I already

know: *he's under the tree*. No matter how long I look,
tracing the paths of grass around the plots, he's missing
like toddler who got bored and wandered off on his own.

St. Anthony of Padua, 1750, Spanish

St. Anthony, Patron Saint of Lost
Things, why are your hands
empty? You stare at the air
around them in wooden-eyed
surprise. Your face is still
young, part tree, part poly-
chrome glaze. Your five
o'clock shadow frames
red lips. But your hands,
St. Anthony, your hands,
only two thumbs and two
fingers remain intact, point
upward—waiting, patient—
with fingernails the size
of a baby's. St Anthony,
you are everywhere for
me: at home on my altar,
in Kiev underground interred,
on a card slipped into my
wallet, helping me find my eye-
glasses in the grass in the side
yard. And yet I'm surprised to see
you here in the plastic case
in Phoenix at the end
of the gallery hall, your hands
aloft, waiting to see who enters.

Note to the Museum Mermaid

to Frederick Judd Waugh's *The Mermaid, 1914-1915*, at the Phoenix Art Museum

Mermaid,

I have lost you, some-
where in the second floor
maze. Turquoise bubbles float up
the wall, released from the copper

and oil, but I cannot find my
way back to your watery gallery where
the submerged dragon, his nostrils flaring, hides
amongst the silvery fish, watching your flesh

whiten the mossy world, his eyes wide as a stalking
cat's, his nose cone-shaped and black-tipped
like a fox. You should wink
at him, dear mermaid,

while I'm wading
back, and remember not to
take your eye off
his steady gaze.

Walking with Angels

Somewhere he stepped, his shoe perhaps sporting
a buckle, his head wearing a wig. Somewhere his soles
pressed the arranged bricks and worn wooden
floors. Occasionally, my footsteps land there, too.

Occasionally, he filled his cup with wine, and his fingerprints,
for which there's never been a matching set, lined the pewter.
Cyrus knows where he's been and might have seen Swedenborg
only yesterday. For me, it's been centuries since

anyone sipped from that cup. Maybe he placed it on the mantle.
Maybe he knocked it off the oak table when his cuff caught
the corner. Maybe he needed no cup, and the wine came
pouring into his mouth directly from heaven.

What I Carry

How to bring a young boy into this shadowy
world when he is full of such light? I offer
options: *You could pray to St. Michael. You could
pray to St. Andrew, your patron saint. Or you could
pray to St. Anthony. He's for kids.* But my go-to
saint is St. Francis: *Make me a channel of your
peace.* But this boy doesn't accept the options
claiming he doesn't know how to pray, can't
even start. And I can't explain what
I know: we only have what we carry.

In the 1970's, St. Brigid's ceiling exposed bluebirds
and naked men hovering in loin cloths. I inspected
the baby-angels' penises weekly. The ceiling was wide
as the sea, and I floated on it buoyed by Russell Robinson's voice,
which commanded we *sing it over!* rocking my seven
year-old body, rattling my ribs, vibrating my arms when
we raised them during the last part of "Our Father,"
and the adults beside me would pull me almost off the floor:

*For thy is the kingdom--and the power--and the glor-y--
For Ev-er.* we sang. *Amen.* Mr. Robinson's voice
has resided inside me ever since, the deep resounding
I have never heard again, not in forty years, and still
his bass voice lives (*Sing it over!*) within me, reminding
me of the lift and lilt of grace and how to manage what I carry.

At 2:33 a.m.

Reading online, I learn that writers and artists can buy
houses in Detroit, my homeland, for the cost of utilities

and insurance and a two-year commitment to stay.
Meanwhile, my husband continues to pull semi-trucks

and backhoes through his sinuses at regular
intervals, affording me these moments of early morning

reflection. My broken foot is showing colors now that
match the Midwestern sunrise—not the fuchsia or water-

melon streaks like here in Albuquerque, where we stay
with family, but the greys and dull purples of swollen rust-

belt days. Writers might move to Detroit for cheap
housing. They might. But so much depends on the sky.

Finally, the Moon

On her 42nd birthday, she drives past bluffs and mesas gliding
east of the sunset that opens like a rose, commanding
curves of gratitude. Three decades as an adult, two divorces,
one unexpected child have driven her to this place where
four lanes thread New Mexico's Badlands, and her life
winds northwest on NM 550. This moment becomes the sky

ahead, expanding bloody reds and fuchsia with yellow
outlining the horizon. She cups this bounty. It is all
before her. It is all behind her. One man in a baggy jacket,
hands shoved into his pockets, walks the shoulder looking
down. He, too, is headed towards the night. After she arrives,
she will transcribe the lines of the road into lines

of a poem and see letters coalesce into words.
She will seek stanzas, experiment with enjambment,
deliberate form. It takes four decades for this
confluence to occur beneath transitory clouds.
Seventy-five miles per hour reveals ideas born
in places: canyon, volcanic rock bed, sealed

into black waves, high plains desert silhouetting
a curled juniper, an absentminded tumbleweed,
and, finally, the moon, blossoming into crescent.

All that Matters

I write SB for a stolen base. K for strikeout.
BB for a walk. I haven't kept score in thirty
years yet I still know to put a thick crosses
where the innings end. In the slump
that is my life right now these little diamonds
bring me home, one brown box for each
at bat, shading out debt and angry spouse,
aching foot and ailing father, arriving
to where there's only one bat and one
ball, and I get to sit behind the backstop
counting every single pitch—the balls
and strikes and passed balls the only way
to measure all that matters in the moment.

Part III: Full

First Words

In 1969, the year of my birth, the *American Heritage Dictionary of the English Language* was published in hardback the color of a paper bag. As a child, when I wanted to know what a word meant, my father told me to look it up. Thumbing through the thousands of pages, letters, symbols and illustrations meant months

and years would pass finding a word between Li and Lo. Only then might I land on *longevity* through the length of chance, the way that my index finger might land on the right town on an unfamiliar map, begging the question: *what's this doing here?* When did this book and I part ways? At least a quarter

century later, sitting in a writer's workshop in Tucson, I spy it above me as close and as far as an angel: the original compass of love that led me straight to words. *The* book—*The Exact One*—right year, proper dun color, spine intact with the cover ragged, just. like. mine. Its layer of dust says that it's lonely, that its crispy pages have remained barely

touched. The book's fatness peers down from the high shelf, tired as a middle-aged mother, and I pull her down from the shelf and hold her cover between my hands, then trace her words under my fingers, pressing pages, dry and soft as aging skin, and we bend towards each other like an old couple in December, sitting across a table, sharing a warm pot of soup.

Old Lesson

Mexico rose wet with ash. Every day,
new words were given to me across counters
and grocery aisles, words like: *¡Mira!* And
justo llegamos. And *no,* which is the same
in both languages, but the vowel comes across
the palette in Spanish, brushing the nose. In
English, it's only a matter of lips. S*olo* works
similarly. In either language, you are alone
(*estás solo*), but in Spanish it's a whisper
and the tongue touching teeth. In English,
the words start the same way but then the jaw
collapses and the throat invades the mouth.
In English, if you are solo, you're simply
alone, but in Spanish, using a different verb,
eres solo, you're not only alone, you're also
unattached, single, and very not married.

The Face at the Bottom

The face at the bottom
of the cup is bowed and wears
eyes, which peer through
round glasses and a nose. When
it blinks, it disappears. Its
grey brows often furrow but twice
last week it winked at me like a child.

Everybody Knows That

Angels live in libraries.
Descending after closing time from the vents and skylights,
gathering at the tables, they read, heads bowed
toward the pages. They don't even whisper. The old
lady librarian's fiery eyes demand peace.

One angel
a month types the new library cards on yellow
cardstock using a gray Underwood. The striking
keys ease the silence.

At the check out
desk young Damien's wings wriggle and flounce,
knocking Cyrus's books to the carpet. *Little Women*
and *Satanic Verses* thud on impact while Cyrus slips
Paradise Lost under his wing and shoves Swedenborg's
Heaven and Hell under a nearby bookcase with his foot. Angel

wings inhibit bending down and Tyree, trying to
help gather the fallen letters, tumbles into a chair. The old
librarian glances up from her copy of *Time* and flames
flash from her irises. Damien tucks
in his velvety feathers. Cyrus shrugs and pats
himself down, checking to be sure that Milton hasn't moved.

Why It Matters

The shadow of the palm
tree paints the side of the math
building, which forms a concrete
cube. The campus architects must
have feared the sun, or the budget didn't

allow for windows. The math
students will need to day
dream without a view
for inspiration. The real tree,
father of the shadow, towers

into the sky twice
as high as the beige cube's top
where tucked inside people
study distance and calculate
why it matters.

At 3:30 a.m.

The early morning angel came
vested in black and grey and quoting
the Koran with *Allah* dancing from his
lips and cloaked in words like *Inshallah* and
Wallah. When he saw my broken foot
he quit reciting and laid his winter

jacket across my outstretched
leg. Only then I realized I was
cold and that I was there
to listen, though I didn't speak
Arabic, and the black-haired angel
had come to slip me back to sleep.

Only Swedenborg Goes to Heaven and Returns

Sissy told me to look out
for the sunset. And I do.
She is right: midsummer,
9 p.m., flying west, the plane
ascends into the sunset,
reaching one layer of dark
blue like I am reaching
heaven, only to increase
altitude and puncture another
layer. Only the pools of lava
lining the horizon show
where the curve of the earth
gives way to the sections of
sky that this plane will never
reach. Flying into heaven this
way, I wonder if I will die
tonight, now, as I write this
on the last leg of a long journey
with my ankles swollen and my
right foot burning and my
sissy left behind in Chicago
after the eight-hour layover,
the head of the plane like
a shark swimming through
the blackening sky, sky, sky.

México Shining

I. Copal Rising

This time México turned north and arrived
  through the sun and stretching across the concrete one

Tuesday afternoon in September. How
rich the word: copal. In the daylight, it smells

of darkness, of Maximon in the cave, an effigy
in striped pants propped against the altar,

surrounded by candles blinking. In the cave,
the copal gives way to *pox*. Hours later, it

enters the mouth, sits on the tongue like fermented
honey, like love that will not leave.

When I close my eyes, the copal becomes the chain
kissing the thurible as Father readies the air.

II. Mé-xi-co Shining

Metl = agave. Xictli = the navel.
Co = within. Agave is the navel

within. The navel
within is made
from agave. Within

agave the navel
forms. México is the agave
is the navel within the agave

and also Metlxictlico,
the center in which
the sweetness forms and thrives.

III. One Day

It all floated towards me at once--copal rising
and México shining from my view at the top

of Toniná. I said, Love, this is it. *Es todo.*
But he was gone. Already

departing, stirring up the sleeping
butterflies as he strode through the grass.

Alone, I had the white and spinning
wings, the day moon, pale,

and arcing acres of green.
I had the sun and the wide,

wide air that tasted blue. I had the new
memory of my love and he, too, came shining.

IV. Red Galactic Moon

On the 27th day of September
in 2011, on 8 Muluc in the Tzolkin
calendar—day of the Red Galactic
Moon—day 12.19.18.13.9 in the long
count, México arrived in New Mexico
as it does daily. This time, blue feathers
fanned out from his head and goat hoof
shakers hugged his calves. He twisted
his inner thigh to touch his skin to the fire,
demonstrating how to burn without singeing.

Smashing the Apple

Andrew slams the beige box
first. Then I wallop the key-
board against the cement wall.
Andrew shouts, "Mama, enter
broke off and so did backspace."
He wants to keep the space
bar. I say, "The point is to
keep nothing." I lean over
and pluck the escape
key from the gravel. This was

the Mac Classic II that carried
me through graduate school
the first time. Somewhere
inside its plastic walls
essays on Hardy, Woolf,
and Joyce grumble, along
with poems over-ripened by ennui.
Maisie used to sit atop the boxy
computer like a grey loaf

of bread and every now and again
drop one fat paw against the cursor,
head bent toward the letters, eyes
more electric than the screen.
This was twenty years ago, which
is twice my son's age on this
Sunday in March when we decide
to wipe the memory clean, no
matter the words left inside.

Letter to Miró

Dear Joan,

I thought I left you
in Spain, but no,
you're here too
in Glendale. On
the wall your little
animals play in red
and green costumes.

Joan, though there
I visited the Sofia
Reina to see you
and waited in line,
here you are
mostly my secret.

Here on campus
most students think
you are a woman,
and those who do
come to admire
the paintings often
miss seeing your
mirthful animals
for Picasso's bull

hanging in agony
to your right. How
can you miss what
you can't even see?
Oh, Joan, your shapes
form glee: eye of pea-
cock. Tail of fish. Spot
of yellow. Hen's black
beak and sleeping dog.

"This is all for you,"
says each lithograph,
here and in Madrid,
every single one, *Todo
para tí,* but I must lean
towards the wall
to hear it: *todo.*
Your offering
for the world in sky

blue. Joan, your
fat black streaks follow
my fingers and I can
touch your lines
and trace your cones and
the cock-eyed rhombus and
the dog's black nose and
feel how the curving red arc
becomes the neck

of hen. I will never see them
all at once—the figures
leaping and swimming
and morphing, becoming
each other, hen to hound,
sea bass to cat paw, cat
paw to mouse ear, mouse
ear to black crossing raccoon
tails, crossing raccoon tails
to this fantastic dream.

Everything Beyond

My first time in New Mexico, before I ever
moved there, we drove north of Taos at sunrise.
My mother and I wound around a narrow road
leading out of town, heading into a dim morning
light I had never seen before—droplets of suspended
sun illuminated poverty, and everything beyond
darkened into silhouettes. Heading toward the Rio Grande
we passed two dogs dead on the road, lying still
and bloodied like actors from a western. The German
Shepherd had blood pooled around his mouth—
a killing so recent, the liquid glistened in the sun.

Somewhere

I.

Somewhere beneath my toes
four cracks refuse to seal, cells
that refuse to clasp their minute fingers

together: red rover, red rover, send the big
toe on over. Somewhere
along my four metatarsals,

four angels are learning to knit
by the light of the rising sun.

II.

The sleeping and the awake lie
side by side like toes topping
the foot—so much easier
to support with all parties

in agreement. Today I rode
Blue for the first
time since she crushed
my foot, each of the four

phalanges snapping like
wish bones. Four
wishes and then I sat
stalled out in a line

of traffic. Anxiety won't
start the engine, but physics
and a well-timed thumb
get her going every time.

Dream of the Husband

You dream again of snow, and I open
the front door in the middle of March
to welcome the jasmine breeze.

The neighborhood cat pounces
on a slash of sunlight and the Airedale
barks, reverberating the table

and the pen against the page. You
dream of snow again, and I wonder
what someone else's dream becomes

for me. When my husband shouts at the man
in the mask to leave his dream, how does he
crawl over the wall into my own imagination?

On Leaving *Don Quixote*

I try to slip it into the drawer beside the lopsided bed,
but it hits with a thud. I am ready to shed this weight
of four hundred years, to drop this quixotic book
that has dominated the last two months of my life. Like with my first
two husbands, I decide to leave, knowing that when I
go, I seldom look back. This was not a decision

I made lightly. I napped on it. And during deliberations, I drank
a glass of Aspall Cider. In a gripping moment of regret, I again skimmed the introduction by
Harold Bloom. But two days prior, I picked up Swedenborg, attracted to the thick pages of his
spiritual diaries enountered in the city where he died. Now it's time
                                        to depart. With limited space, something must
remain, so even though Spain arrives tomorrow, I cannot carry extra pounds.

May the next lucky person who sleeps in this tilted bed
reach into the drawer for Gideon and find Cervantes waiting instead.

After Words and Books

When the great bird was carrying us home and the thunderstorm hovered
over Phoenix, I slept hungry for the void. The rain marked the plastic
windows and I kept my head against my husband's shoulder and slipped
in and out of the clouds the same way the rain came and went. There was
nothing—not even the figment of an image to dream, nothing but shushing
vibrations and the thin jet of air above my head, fingering my hair.

PART IV: WANING

About My Father

Day 1—After Falling

After falling, he lay there for hours during
Detroit's coldest winter in over 100 years.
While he waited, maybe by parked cars, perhaps
besides mailboxes

or next to an ice-sealed bush,
the fluid in his lungs formed two wintery seas.
No one told me what happened until
my mother returned from South Africa
and she called to share this
news about the man whom she divorced

two decades ago. Why had no one
interrupted the 84-degree day in
Phoenix with such cold?

Day 2—Sometimes the Impact

Sometimes the impact is delayed.
After a dinner of chicken and warm
apples, my throat tightens against
the sweetness and grief clenches my voice

box, finding me every-
where I reside: in the TV room
easy chair, at my desk. on the left side
of the bed where I lie, imagining
him fallen

in the snow, wondering *where are his angels?*
Why are they leading him away so soon? I tap the
silver angel pendant hanging from my chain.
Grief will ring my throat.

Day 3—Water

She calls and asks if I remember him
drinking water. Coffee regular? Yes. Water? No.
I had the last weekend of his life without his needing
a walker, and we listened to Gershwin in concert

together, and showing him my campus made him beam.
A beer? Sometimes. But never, ever water. *Remember*
she said (not your mother, but your sister) *how he used*
to pop his vitamins into his mouth and put his mouth

under the sink and run the tap? He collected only
what would push the pills down his throat. One time
he caught me – I was just tall enough to stretch my neck
over the sink to mouth the falling water. He caught
me midstream and snapped, *Stop that. You'll chip a tooth.*

Even Angels

Thanks to them, nothing
I lose cannot be found
except what is swallowed

by the sea. Even angels
avoid great depths—
blue wet cannot accommodate

feathers. Soggy feathers
don't serve. Even a human
being can understand that.

Atropos, Or the Fates, 1820-1823

Franciso, I like your name. Or
rather I like to say it: Fran-cis-
co, to hear each distinct syllable
and feel my tongue begin the word

and my mouth take over, stopping in
Oh. By the end you wouldn't
have heard me or anyone say it—
pronounce the vowels as carefully

as you painted the finery on
Las Meninas. Fran-cis-co – one
syllable for each Fate that you
painted: Atropos, Lachesis &

Clotho, who clutch scissors, a lens
and wind the fateful thread.
And the floating
figure. Is this you? The largest

shape in the painting, curled in
upon himself with the left leg in
prominent view. Fates, Francisco,
the unavoidable mess your country

made. What could you do
in your deafness but depict yourself
in untethered blackness just as the sign
points out, "The one

figure that doesn't follow
the iconography," the largest
of all, the foot of your deafness
floating, facing front, toes

grey, hands holding the brush behind
your back, your head, including your stone
ears, wrapped in a velvet scarf, unable to hear
me utter Francisco, Francisco, Francisco.

Maybe This…Over Here

Toward the mountains where the blue
sky is wrapped in a horizon of haze
the brown cattle bend to the ground
facing south. I imagine these western
high plains not full of Indians, cattle, horses
or buffalo, but filled with angels as they are
now, wings bobbing and waving
in the April wind, feathers combing
and braiding the air like fingers. Maybe
this was where to find my father's angel

on that subzero day outside Detroit and
the angels belonging to the passengers
on Flight 17 while it plummeted over Ukraine
and the angels of the two headless journalists—
here on the blowing plains of the Navajo rez—
a chorus of angels, a passel, a gaggle, a herd,
a pack, a swarm, a murder, a flock of them—
plentiful but far-flung like sunflowers
or stars far from the worries of their humans.

The Conference of Cats

I know when I enter the kitchen for my morning
coffee that the ring of crouching cats doesn't signify
a start-of-the-day debriefing. I am prepared to meet
a stumpy-tailed lizard. Instead, I bend down
to find a sparrow smaller than my palm.
He's had a bad morning. How

do you touch a living thing about to die? Forgetting
I'm in my underpants, I scoop him up in a towel
and place him in the V of the mulberry tree
outside. I know I've not stopped death. But
for a little while (tiny, really) I halted the conference,
which will reconvene in the front yard momentarily.

Finding Sam

My mother remembers me
in the kitchen on Graham
talking to Sam on the phone.

I remember we often talked
sitting on the yellow metal monkey
bars. I listened while Sam told me
stories of shark fishing in Florida,
and his mom's job as an ER nurse
granted him stories of six year-old
gore. It was 1976. In twelfth grade,

Sam drove us to Spanish class daily
crosstown. Even in the flat green
world of Dearborn, MI, he had a South-
westerner's sense of time. I got a B
that semester for being tardy
every day. In 2014,

my mother and I share a sandwich
at Luci's in Phoenix. I say,
"Mom, I found Sam. His office is two
or three miles from here." So we drive
west down Bethany Home and turn
left on 7th Street. Two miles down
a shiny building the color of a penny
reflects palm trees and parked cars.

I make a U and we drive
to pick up Andrew from school.
Thirty-eight years later, it's enough
to know Sam's behind the mirrored
walls seeing patients and perhaps
watching the same sunset fling the orange
evening into ribbons across the sky.

Two Guns

I. West Bound

We are quiet on the freeway and now there is nothing
to say but to watch the sun ease down the horizon,
leaving a wavy pink wake. We have traveled over four
hundred miles after working a full day. We pass Two

Guns, Arizona, and now, work ended for one day,
there is nothing to do but note Mt. Humphries growing
closer. We have been gliding under grey

since we left, and the end of the cloud
front hovers between us and the mountain. When we
arrive beneath the star-filled sky, we will be halfway.

II. East Bound

The same stretch of abandoned train cars line I-40.
Whose day will be filled with hooking up to their loneliness
and pulling them home? The fourth car explodes
with graffiti: HOLLA. The H, taller than a grown man, leans

into the O which bounces into the double L which sidles
up to the peaking A. My mother-in-law, refusing to believe
that phones are now mobile, calls near Gallup and thinks

we are at home. But the land turns into reservation and more
emptiness as we point the car north for the final leg, and the call
drops as her voice rises and her hollering engulfs the night.

CGI

After I show him the online video that ends
with the fairy in the apple tree, my stepson

shrugs and says, "CGI." And when I don't
understand, he grumbles, "Computer Generated

Image." But I need that fairy with his black
legs dangling between lacy wings the way

I need the trail of feathers in the backyard
not to lead to the lifeless dove, the way

that when I'm writing in the library
I need to imagine Cyrus and Damien above

me stirring up the dust motes and floating
in the sails of the skylight, releasing

words and letting them drift down and settle
onto my pages one tired lonely letter at a time.

Carrying It All

I find myself carrying a fifty-pound duffle up 165
steps (which, the sign claims, is equal to 12.5 flights
of stairs) because the lift is broken. The bustle underground
delights, the motion brewing beneath, the towering
escalators which lift and lower humans in lines, the wind
whooshing, ruffling scarves and blowing back jackets.
All this delight occurring beneath the soil, down there. Until
the delight is no longer light and this business of carrying
the burden beneath needs someone to bear
witness. I want to travel light like tall John, packing
only a small shoulder bag, allowing my length alone
to fill this world and not my shoes, t-shirts or books,
not my stacks of empty journals or my Levi's,
which have been increasing in size almost
annually. I only seem to widen in this world,
pack on weight around my hips and thighs and belly.
I never seem to grow any taller. And the young man,
the one who didn't let me decline his help, the one
who simply grabbed one strap and claimed half my
burden as we ascended the 165-step spiral, the remaining
six flights with my heart hammering too hard for me
to hug or thank him before he eased through the shiny
turn stall and into the light—that guy? the one
with wings? I want to mention him, too.

The Results, c. 1810-1820

Following the Napoleanic Wars, Francisco
Goya arrived too one day in Glendale, hanging
next to a William Hogarth engraving, *Analysis
of Beauty*, and two of Honore Daumier's political
cartoons. Plate 72 of Goya's 80-print series *Disasters of
War* reminds us that dark-winged creatures, like hungry
cats, crouch on the belly of a man lying prone. How
the feathers stir the air around him! The sparrow on top
the palm tree sees only his forest of fronds and knows
nothing of the feline stationed forty feet beneath.

The Goodness of Waiting

Walking back from Rickett's Park
I came across my body. Under the dark
and heavy sky I found it where it had been waiting
for years. Putting it on there between the empty
baseball diamonds, I felt the familiar tugs—a bit too snug

in the hips, too tight in the chest and full
in the belly--but still familiar and easy. Finally inside
myself again, I found an empty dugout and turned towards
the field, watching no players, umpires, or fans, no cheering crowds
or disputed calls, just me reveling in the comfort of finally sliding home.

Another Beginning

I never held a baby
bird before. I removed
the gloves and used both
hands to cup

the airiness. I was supposed
to keep my eye on
it. My mother says
I entered this world clutching

a sparrow in each fist. The doctor
yanked me out with forceps.
I was supposed to keep an eye

on the bird with the gaping
yellow beak so it wouldn't die. But it died
decades ago and I still can't look its way.

Easter Poem, 2016

Christ knew it
was coming, too. Good
Friday, my husband

came over and mentioned he was
filing for divorce, that a psychic
told him that I was waiting for him

to do this and that I was holding
him back. Imagine my
surprise despite the psychic

involvement. Christ knew
it was coming, but did
that knowledge only

increase the burden
he hauled up Golgotha?
Is this what he balanced with

the cross aloft? Does knowing
it's the end eradicate the ending?
When Lazarus enters

our story from behind the giant
boulder, does he teach Jesus
how to begin again?

Arriving the Perfect

And then, some time soon, the next
life, the perfect one beyond
bickering with the cat about the empty food
bowl (she always wins), beyond
the bills and calculating taxes, beyond
days with wind that stirs
up dust that must be later wiped, beyond
elms that lose their leaves and litter
the floor in December, yes, just beyond
here and over there, round
the next enjambment and beneath
the final stanza break, a slight
pause, then past the nightmare of the train
that startles you awake and into
the poem, beyond the husband
in the other house snoring on his own
pillow in his own bed, almost right

now arriving, the perfect—

At 4:15 a.m.

And the cat is busy
and why not? Someone is out
there accelerating down Olive Ave.,
driving the machines which provide the sound-
track for my dreams. Why not expect
to be fed at 4 a.m.? Then full,

why not stretch into the green throw
blanket and bathe? The dog
will not stir, not even peek one fuzzy
ear over the blanket once. He knows
the truth about 4 a.m. and heaven
knows someone in the house must seek it.

Looking at the Dead

It wasn't hard to look at my dead
father. I use *dead* without
euphemism for whatever
part of him remained was
no longer living. He looked skeletal
already with his broad
forehead and his large
teeth hiding like quiet mountains
behind his lips. But his eyes
would not close, would keep cracking
open, his eyelids creeping
apart, his irises
no longer blue. I wasn't
afraid to touch what I had loved
touching when it lived, my father's
face, trim white beard in front
of a small chin, thick lips and his bald
pate, which only ever asked
for a warm palm to rest on. I wasn't
afraid to look and I'm not afraid
to remember but I cannot
equate my vacant father with
his being gone. I remind myself
daily, "He is dead," so that
I can recall. But gone where?

If I could imagine him there, resting,
stretched six feet long across the living-
room floor wherever he
now resides—just a cat
nap after dinner while watching
the news—perhaps I could move
his image there, like some
kind of imagination UHaul, and carry
him over to The Next Place in a worn
out orange and white vehicle where

the brakes start late and the visor
knocks against your skull and smacks
into your lap when you try to pull it
down against the glare. Where is
my father now that he has set?
Unlike Jesus or the sun, he
will not rise again. Where
is my father? Gone.

The Center of Love

"In birds, the red blood cells still contain a nucleus."
--*BrokenWing Chronicles*

Imagine when I realized this constant
panicky feeling was missing my father was life
without my father, even though for years he
was over there by the big lakes under clouds
while I lived in the desert under sun. Imagine
for weeks my heart was a sparrow's – tiny
chambers though which larger-than-usual
cells must flow keeping the nucleus tucked

inside. Imagine driving through a suburban
parking lot with Pharrell's song "Happy"
playing when the answer to *What is different?*
What is different? finally comes as easily as
shutting off the radio. This is different this being
without—this speaker without a song. This twittering
without feathers. This heart pumping blood
without nuclei, the center of love simply gone.

Acknowledgments

"An Essay on Refraction." *Four Chambers: The Heart of Literature.* Issue 2. October 2014.

"Everything Beyond" and "Finally, the Moon." *200 New Mexico Poems.* 2012. https://200newmexicopoems.wordpress.com/category/kimberly-mathes/

"Grace," "It Must Be Something Else," "Two Guns." *The Drunken Boat.* Fall 2013/Winter 2014. http://www.thedrunkenboat.com/kimberlymathes.html

"It Must Be Something Else." *Poetry for the Spirit.* 2009.

CPSIA information can be obtained
at www.ICGtesting.com
Printed in the USA
FFOW02n1523140517
35580FF